Damage
Noted: _5/99 Crayon_

To my mother, Anna, whose constant faith and love kept me going;
to all the Black people who encouraged me and helped me; to Africa—
the reaffirmation of all my strongest beliefs in Black humanity

Black Pilgrimage

TOM FEELINGS

Lothrop, Lee & Shepard Co. | New York

*T*he first right of a people who want to be free is the right to define their own reality.

Bill Strickland.

I choose to depict the things that I love most.

I thought of submitting this book without words, letting the art speak for itself. However, to aspiring Black artists, and to Black people as a whole, my experience and ideas may be of some value. For this reason, I have offered some background to work I have done since 1960, when I first started drawing from life in the Black community.

From 1960 to 1964 that's practically all I did. I drew in Brooklyn and the Black South. In 1964 I took my sharpened eye and skill to Africa—and now, what I have been given by the heart and soul of the Black community both here and abroad, I give back to you.

I grew up in Bedford-Stuyvesant, a Black community in Brooklyn. Right outside my door on Putnam Avenue were the streets and kids, neighbors, friends, stores, churches, pool halls, bars, and schools, the bright lights of Fulton Street and Nostrand Avenue. There I was initiated into life, and that neighborhood became the first true inspiration for my work.

7

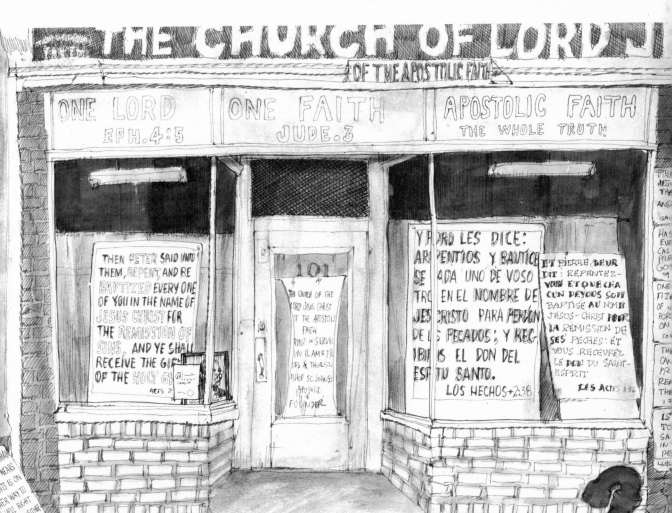

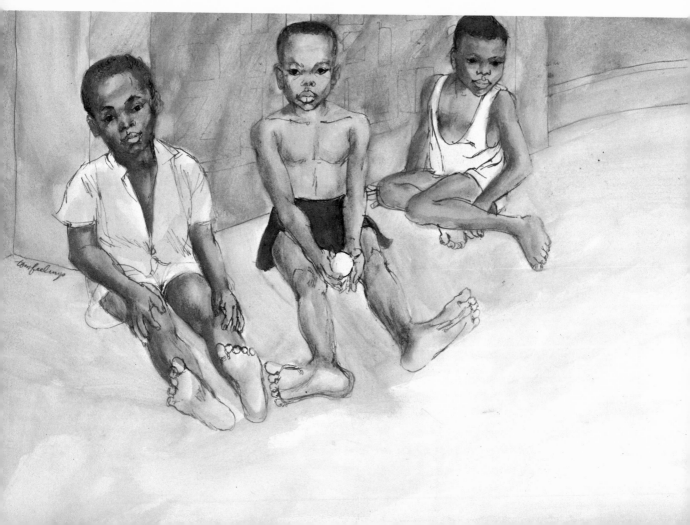

In the late 1950's, the time of a growing, active Black protest, I got out of the Air Force and entered an art school in New York to study painting and illustration.

I soon learned that nothing in my art training dealt with the realities of the life from which I came. We were told that we should paint the things we felt most deeply about, but that encouragment was not meant for me. When I brought in Black subject matter, I either got the cold shoulder or was told that I was "overly sensitive."

One day in an art history class, I asked the lecturer, "Weren't there any Black artists of significance?" "No," he said. "Well, what about African Art?" I asked. "That's in a different class. That's primitive art," the lecturer replied. I walked out of the class. I *had* to reject a history that did not include me.

11

Soon afterwards, I started some projects of my own. The first was a comic strip called "Tommy Traveler in the World of Negro History." I felt there was a need for Black heroes. The story centered around a young Black boy who couldn't find enough books on Black History in his public library. Someone told him about a Black doctor who had his own private collection. Tommy went to the doctor's house, and the doctor let him read there. Tommy read and, each time, fell asleep dreaming himself into the story he'd just read. Tommy was really me.

I sold the strip to a Harlem newspaper, *The New York Age*, where it ran for a year. At the same time I did a complete comic book on Crispus Attucks, former slave and hero at the Boston Massacre of 1770, and walked around for seven months trying to sell it. Some years later the Educational Heritage Group in Yonkers bought it, and included it in their children's section on Negro History.

12

Around 1960, I began taking my pad, pencil, and pen wherever I went. I felt a need to put everything down before it changed, while it was changing. So I went into the bars, schools, homes, and streets I knew so well. Today's Black Poetry is right to the point, reflecting just what is being said by the brothers and sisters in the streets, just as they say it. I tried to do the same thing in my drawings.

13

Sometimes I would stand on the corner with unemployed Black men. Even though I was going to art school, I was unemployed too. I had no better a chance of getting a job than they did—not if I continued to focus on Black people.

Things were changing in the Black world in the last months of 1960. Several nations were now independent; others were on their way. The Afro-American's negative concept of Africa was slowly changing. The image I had once drawn of two Black men waiting under a drier for a hair-straightening "process" was fading away.

At this time I joined what was to my mind the first organization to support the positive idea that Black is beautiful and that Africa is our home. It was the African Jazz Art Society of Harlem, the pioneers of the "natural" look. The group lauded the teachings of the Honorable Marcus Garvey, who advanced the theory of Africa for the Africans at home and abroad. Garvey founded the movement that believed Black people should return to Africa, their ancestral homeland, to help **18** build and restore it to its highest potential.

It was the first and only group I have ever chosen to join. The instinctive feelings I had always had and the vague ideas I had wanted to believe in became crystalized when Cecil Brathwaite, the president spoke of us as a people who were African and should be proud of it. We defined our own standards and embraced our African heritage.

One of the unique expressions of the group was a Black fashion show entitled "Naturally 61." In 1962, it took to the road. I traveled with the show from Detroit to Chicago, and to all the Black communities that opened their doors. Today, a walk through any Black community will testify to the positive effect the show had on our people.

I left art school in 1961, with a portfolio filled with my best work—99 percent Black. Most magazines and book publishers just weren't interested. "Don't you draw white people?" they asked. "Your scope seems limited; why don't you be practical and include more white people? You shouldn't place so much emphasis on race. It just shows that you are different."

Even when illustrations of Black people were needed, the assignments generally went to white illustrators, who knew nothing of the Black images or experiences. When I did get assignments they were usually stories about depressive situations.

20

Fortunately, two Black magazines encouraged me during this period, and exposed my work to Black communities across the country. They were *The Liberator* and *Freedomways*. Most of the works they published were drawings from life.

Spiritually, Black writers gave me strength, too. Even though I knew what I was doing was right, their work reaffirmed the validity of the Black experience, and kept me from feeling isolated.

While I was in art school, I had worked at various jobs, and it had been hard. Now that I was out of school, I wanted at least a year of free-lancing. I was afraid that if I took a job in an art studio I would be forced into a white mold before I had a chance to form my own way of working. Because of the faith and support of my mother, who allowed me to remain in her home (though I supplied little money to the household), I was able to start free-lancing in 1961.

21

At first I got very few jobs, so there was plenty of time to go out into the streets, drawing, sharpening my skills and eye. I put this increasing perception into any work that I did get. But nothing gave me as much satisfaction as ending up with six or seven good pieces at the end of a full day of drawing.

During all that time my mother never applied any pressure on me to get a "regular job." I'm sure she felt some pressure herself from neighbors. If I was a working artist, why was I home so much and in the streets of Bed-Stuy drawing? The people who paid money for art weren't interested in drawings of Black people.

In 1962, I took my portfolio to the art director at *Look* magazine at what happened to be a good moment. They had planned a feature article called "The Negro in the U.S.A." He had asked me if I would go to the South. I jumped at the offer! I had visited the South when I was fourteen, too young to appreciate the full meaning of the life style of Black people there. I had always wanted to go back. So, soon I was off to New Orleans.

There I stayed at a Black hotel. When the two women who commanded the kitchen heard I was from New York and had never even tasted gumbo, they turned me into a special project. Day after day, they filled me up with marvelous stews—crab, pork, beef, shrimp, and spices of all kinds, cooked in one pot. The people I met there were like that, warm to me, warm to one another. The hotel owner invited me to eat with his family and talked to me about his voter-registration work.

25

I roamed the streets of the city's Black section just drawing and soaking up the sun. The children had a special appeal for me, and as I drew, they were quick to respond. They seemed different from kids in Bed-Stuy. There was more warmth, openness and happiness in these faces. And I had never noticed such a variety of skin colors—red-brown, blue-black, yellow.

26

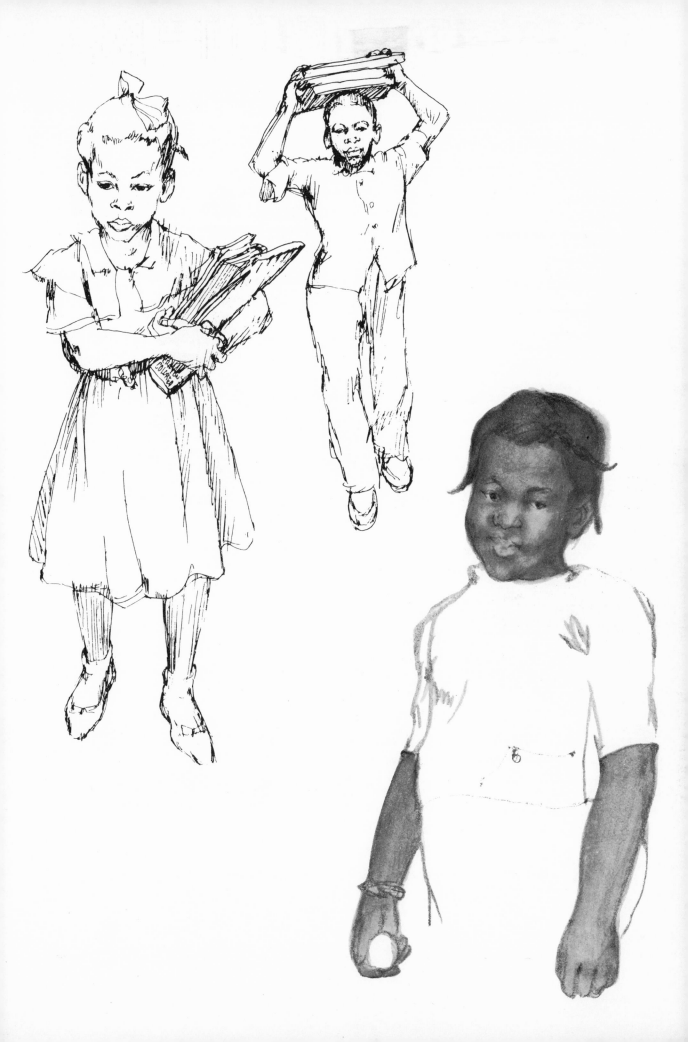

The drawings I had done in the North showed little happiness, and I began to wonder if this was just my own outlook on Black life or if that was the way it really was. From this short trip I got the feeling of a slower, less hurried life; it was the start of my search for a reflection of the warmth lying just beneath the unhappiness in the faces of most Black people I had seen. It was like something I had always known but had forgotten.

I am aware that Black people in the South do not control their own lives any more than they do in the North. I know now that what I saw and felt in the Black South had a lot to do with the sun, the open air and the food. It was more than the children's faces that made me feel as I did. It was the whole atmosphere. I realized this with a shock when

28

I came back to Brooklyn and looked at the faces again, right outside my door on Putnam Avenue. They were the same faces. Had I really looked at them before? Had I seen the beauty in them? And if I hadn't, growing up with them, drawing them, who had? I felt a driving responsibility to put it all on paper, because, as far as I knew then, no one else was going to draw what I was living and feeling every day.

32

It was summertime, in Brooklyn. Children were all out on the streets. I'd walk over to a group and say, "I want to do a drawing of you." Sometimes they'd take a stiff, self-conscious pose, and I wouldn't really start drawing. Then after about five minutes they'd forget I was there and relax. That's what I'd been waiting for, and I'd start drawing quickly. The restless ones made me work hard because they didn't want to sit still at all. Sometimes I would do drawings without their knowing it, from across a street or on a train or bus. Little by little, I began to be caught up in what was in front of me, forgetting sometimes where I was, just responding to what I felt.

34

I chose children as subjects because they had had less time to be exposed to the pain of being Black in a white country, and because they reflect the best in us before it is changed or corrupted.

Soon drawings began to flow easily. At times I didn't know what I had put down until I got back home at the end of the day. Then I might add a wash, or cut out whole sections that took away from what I was trying to say, or what the drawing was saying to me. I began to play down *accuracy* for an overall *feel*. In some cases I would exaggerate, to point up some important feature. I was beginning to *see* what I felt. And I tried to show the children, through my work, the effect they had on me.

36

I hoped that their parents would see in these pictures, reflections of the beauty in themselves. Black adults have learned to hide their feelings, but children show it all—joy, sorrow, discouragement, defiance—that is what I tried to capture. But I was sometimes terribly depressed. From the time they were born, as I knew only too well, these kids had two strikes against them, and they would soon find that out. Their frustrations would grow and grow. As they matured, shadows would fall across the fresh open beauty of their faces.

38

I started going to public schools in Bedford-Stuyvesant to show my drawings, and encourage the children to draw themselves. The younger children were usually excited by just the idea that a Black artist had come to the school to show them pictures of children like themselves in familiar surroundings. But the older the child, the more they asked about "how much money" I made. I didn't want to project myself as a symbol of success to them. I was having a hard time, and was definitely not a success in this country's terms. What I wanted to do was to encourage the children to draw the things that surrounded them and to stress how important that activity was.

40

One day in a classroom the kids were excited and liked the drawings, except for one little eight year-old girl who sat in the back. I asked her why she didn't look at the pictures. She said she didn't want to, because they were "ugly."

"They're pretty little Black children, like you," I said.

"Ain't nothin' Black pretty," she answered angrily.

Afro-American Child's Lament

Ghana boys
Nigerian boys
Kenya boys
Liberian boys
They all look like me
They have problems too, I know
But being Black
In their own native land
Is not one of them.

Ruth Duckett Gibbs

It was then that I said to myself, "What's the use of going to one class at a time, when the children need books—lots of them, in their hands, books with positive Black images." I had no means of putting out such books. At the same time, I was determined to go on with my work. I had to go someplace where Black children did not think themselves ugly. I had to go to the true source of Black people—Africa.

42

From Ruth Duckett Gibbs' *Black Is the Color,* Center for Media Development, Inc., 1972. By permission of the publishers.

You say you ain't left nothing in Africa?
Why, you left your mind *in Africa.*
Malcolm X

In 1964, I left for Africa—where I did not have to compromise my identity, change my subject matter, or have it questioned.

The country I chose to go to was Ghana. Since 1957, when Ghana became independent under President Kwame Nkrumah, it had been in the forefront of the fight for African independence and a unified Africa. President Nkrumah welcomed the skills of Black people from America and the Caribbean. When I read about a large printing press Ghana had built in the new industrial area known as Tema, and heard that the government intended to publish its own books, I felt this might be a chance to work for the benefit of a Black country. I soon discovered I was not the only one who felt that way. When I arrived, there were many African-Americans already there.

In Ghana, I lived one of the most valuable experiences of my life—working for an all-Black nation as staff illustrator for the Ghana Government Publishing House, and for the first time, as part of a majority.

43

One of the first things that struck me when I went into the streets and villages to draw, was the glow in the faces. It was a glow that came from within, from a knowledge of self, a trust in life, or maybe from a feeling of being part of a majority in your own world.

I had seen this same glow in the faces of very young Black children in America, the ones who hadn't yet found out that they were considered "ugly."

My basic beliefs were confirmed. Despite our conditions in the West, the Black strength and beauty had survived to a great extent.

44

They had come from our beginnings in Africa. All my innermost feelings about the beauty of the Black people I had known came to life, and I was happy.

Some mornings, half asleep, I'd hear voices talking and laughing outside the house where I was living. The voices, their tone, were as familiar as those I'd heard on Putnam Avenue. Waking up, I'd realize I was in Ghana. And though the voices spoke an unfamiliar language, somehow I had a pretty good idea of what they were saying.

45

Some of my impressions of West Africa will remain with me forever. The sense of family, the close relationship between mother and child was wonderful to see. The small child travels everywhere with the mother, on her back. African families are large and all the members are responsible to one another. This extended family gives the little ones a sense of security. As they grow older, each child has his own chores and they take to these responsibilities eagerly.

I was amazed at the children's thirst for knowledge; they will read anything they can get their hands on. I spent hours in the libraries just watching and drawing the children at study.

46

I chose this little girl to draw because she represents what I would most like to remember about West Africa. She has all the warmth and spirit I so longed to see in Black children in America. I knew that spirit was in the young Black children at home, but it was buried deep under layers of frustration and alienation. I saw none of this in the faces of children I drew in Ghana, and I do not feel I "read something into" the faces. As soon as I saw them I knew what I had came there for . . . to reaffirm a feeling I had deep within me that this is where the warmth and strength must have originated: the knowledge of knowing *who* you are and *where* you come from—that you have the security of an extended family. It's a way of looking at life. As someone once said, "Africa turns all knowledge into a living experience." Once you have seen that, it cannot be taken away from you.

47

And the beauty of women—the long cloth they wear touching the ground—is unforgettable. Sometimes they wrap cloth high about their head. Sometimes they go with their heads uncovered, revealing braided hair pulled tightly back. For so long I had seen the faces of Black women in America with straightened hair falling over their forehead. Now I could see eyes, foreheads, ears—wonderful ears that seemed to have been hidden from view for years. Braided hair revealed to me the liveliness of the African face.

The women are proud and show it in the way they walk—their chin up, looking you straight in the eye—moving gracefully, with the elegance of women who know who they are.

There were many new things for my eyes to feast on—the palm trees in the warm sun, and dusty pastel-colored roads—all the wonderful colors of Africa. I had to change my whole palatte, use more vivid colors, and put more light into my paintings.

The warm weather had a special effect on me. It was similar to my experience in the Black South, the feeling that I had been there before, and I know it had something to do with the land, with knowing that this was the place where my people had always been. There in Africa, with my feet in that soil, I could feel the thousands of years **48** of tradition and culture and a communication with my ancestors.

I am an *African*, and I know now that Black people, no matter in what part of the world they may live, are one African people. And in terms of natural resources and potential, and a culture that built the base of humanity, we belong to the richest continent on earth—Africa.

50

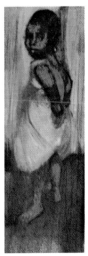

In Ghana I met and worked with many African-Americans: writers, teachers, artists, electricians, plumbers, and architects —all finding a need and an outlet for their skills. There was much building going on. Plumbing and electrical wiring were needed for the large government state building, the Tema printing works, and many other projects. For the first time I came into contact with Black people from America who had the same basic values I did. We developed a close relationship and deep concern for one another.

All of us took an interest in everything that affected the country, the first independent Black country in the new era. I even read the National Budget Report. I felt that my skills were helping in the development of the country, so everything, including its politics, was

54 important to me.

One African-American who came to Ghana during my stay was a brother named Curtis. About twenty-nine, he had fought in Korea, worked at odd jobs and finally worked in the Post Office, where he had saved up money for the trip. Unlike other Black Americans in Ghana, he had no profession or special skills.

"This ain't New York City," one of the brothers said to Curtis. "See that Ghanaian out there with that pick. He gets six shillings a day! That's seventy-eight cents. You can't live off that."

"One thing I learned in my life," Curtis told him, "is not to *panic,* and man, you're trying to make me panic."

I took Curtis to the market, where women in stalls cook and sell foods: beef on coconut leaves, boiled eggs, garden eggs, stews, and groundnut sauce with rice. At night people come out to walk about, and buy their evening meal in the flickering light of oil lamps.

58

Curtis was already talking about selling his return ticket. Now he pointed to some market women selling peanuts, plantains, and bread. "How much is that stuff?" he asked. "A couple of pennies each," I told him. "Man!" he said. "I could make it here for a lon-n-g time, and sleep on the ground!"

At one of the open-air night clubs in Accra, where Ghanaians come to drink beer and dance to the rhythms of the "High Life" band, Curtis just sat watching, and listening to the rhythms. "Oh, man!" he said finally. "All this—and the moon too. I love Ghana!"

It's a beautiful thing when a Black man from America who never had any of the things we are told are necessities can come to Africa and *live*. **59**

I had gone there with no intention of ever leaving. But Nkrumah's government was overthrown by pro-Western forces, and I was told my office was part of Nkrumah's propaganda machinery. It was the first to be closed down, and I was forced to leave.

Just before I climbed into the jet, one face stood out in the mass at the departure gate with a definite African glow. It was Curtis. He held up two fingers in a "V" for victory. It was his way of saying, "Until you come back home, so long for now."

I had been away two years, and when I got back to the States I found change, mostly expressed in a new Black consciousness. There were "poverty programs" and government money floating around, for assistance of that kind, but I knew that was because of the rebellion in the cities rather than any basic change in America. I saw Black people, especially young ones, wearing their hair natural. Identification with Africa was high. I got the feeling that maybe these young people would not tolerate the same kind of treatment that their parents had.

60 I began drawing again, some from life, but not as much as before. I did a series at a center for unwed mothers, and another series of

Brooklyn children at a summer recreation center. Then my time began to be filled with assignments to illustrate books, at first African stories and the stories about children in the American Black community.

The first book I illustrated had an African setting, and I felt that line drawings would not say enough. I had spent hours in Africa soaking up the African sun, and the contrast between black skin and hot white sun stayed with me. I wanted Black children in America to feel that same delightful contrast. So I began to work in tissue paper, blending line with black tones against stark and subtle whites, breathing more life into the pictures.

At first it was exciting doing these books because I believed that they would reach the hands of Black children, give them positive Black images, and encourage other young Black artists to do what I was doing. In a small way I was helping, I thought, to save them from the experience of my generation and all those before me, of having only white images to measure themselves against. But after the tenth book, I began to doubt if this was really what was getting across to them. All of the books were by white writers, and I had to turn down a number of stories because the writers just didn't know anything about the Black experience or were propagating a white view of Black life. I felt that was more damaging to Black children than reissuing *Little Black Sambo*. The racism was far subtler, and more insidious. Nevertheless, the books I turned down were printed anyway, illustrated by white artists. Why, I asked myself, are so many books about Black people, especially for children, suddenly pouring forth now, after so many years of silence on the subject? There were many reasons, of course, but the main one was the profit motive.

62

But why were there so few books by Black writers and artists? The scarcity must have led readers, and especially Black readers, to think that few Black writers, artists, and editors were capable.

The same publishers who showed no interest in Black life in the mid-1960's considered that they were "rewarding" the few Black artists and writers who had managed to survive to this point. We were to be the "exceptional Negroes." There can only be a few "exceptions," and their very rarity implies that the rest lack either the talent or the ambition.

The truth is that we became Black artists in spite of the system, not because of it. I am thankful that I developed my skills before Black books were being published, and that I expanded my feelings of Black consciousness in Africa and was, therefore, able to bring Black children a little more. I saw Black people in Africa doing things together, things I had never seen in America, and I knew what Black people could do on their own.

I know there are Black artists in America who have something important to say in their own way. There always were and always will be; but they have been made "invisible." We must learn from the mistakes of the past, so that we won't end up going through a second Reconstruction Period, or another Harlem Renaissance, with the publishing of our writing and art depending almost entirely upon the whims of a white publishing establishment, or an art patron, or a changing white readership. If we want to hold onto what is ours and not see it distorted and corrupted, *we* must lay the ground *now* so that we direct the recording of it, the telling of it, the writing of it, the publishing and distributing of it ourselves.

The talent that we possess does not belong to us. It was passed down to us from our ancestors, and they who can best express what our ancestors gave us have the most responsibility to pass this message on to the living and the unborn, so that it can live forever.

65

From *When the Stones Were Soft: East African Fireside Tales* by Eleanor Heady. Illustrations copyright © 1968 by Tom Feelings. Reprinted by permission of Funk & Wagnalls, Inc.

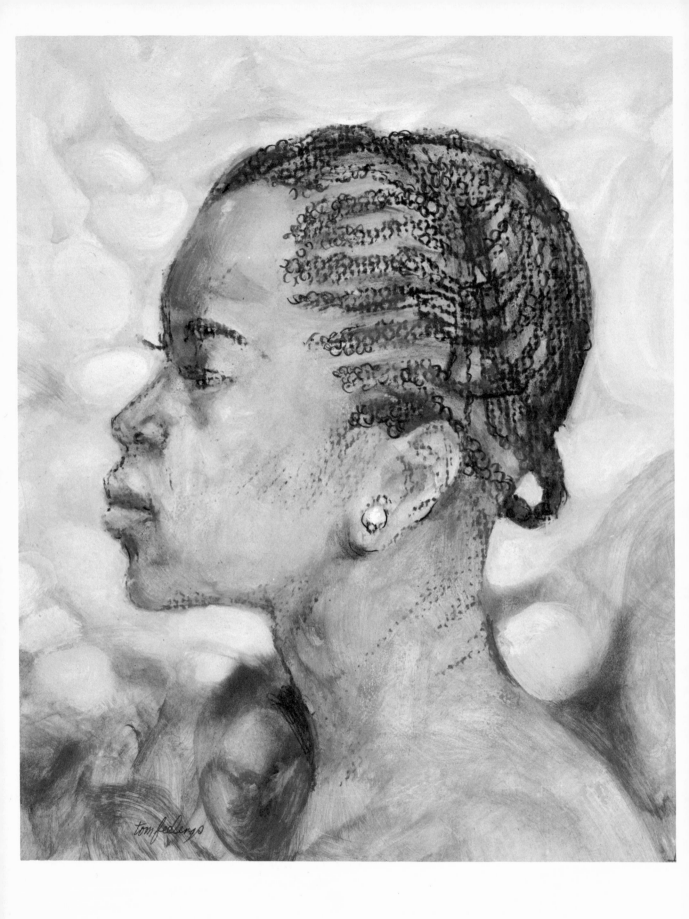

I wanted a large number of my people to see my work, because the things I do are for and about them. The larger masses of Black people never go to art galleries or museums. And why should they? There is nothing there that reflects their experience. Traditionally in America, art has been the possession of the privileged few. Even now, Black art is seen by an elite group, not by the common Black man. I would like to see Black art within the reach of all the people.

Work by Black artists reproduced in the form of prints, posters, cards, and books links the artist to his people and links artist to artist. People who cannot afford to buy original paintings can often afford the same piece of work reproduced as note paper, a poster, a card, a book or a film. It then becomes functional art, accessible to more people. Black poets and writers are doing this now with small magazines that are produced by Blacks and sold for a small price or given away.

In the African tradition, art is not separate from daily life, as it is in the Western sense. It is part of it. Museums house dead objects. African art functions as a part of life. A hand-carved jewel box, a door, or a spoon becomes a beautiful but useful object, not just something to hang up and admire. An African mask is worn during a ritual that includes music and dancing, in which the whole community takes part.

The Western concept of art-for-art's sake, adopted by a Black artist, leads him away from his people, who are trapped in the concept that an art work loses its prestige and money value if it is mass-produced. He finds his work reaching no one but the buyer.

Black artists must rethink the whole idea of "art." Their work must be given back to the people it comes from. The visual arts must be fused with the rest of our art forms—poetry, drama, dance, and music —in order to give direction and life-giving force to Black people.

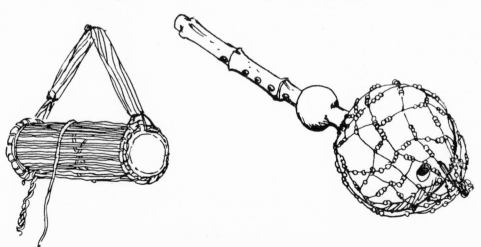

Once the artist has decided on this, he will direct his work toward the Black community and away from white-owned galleries and individual patrons. He will stop picketing museums to include more Blacks in their collections. After all, aren't there enough stolen African masterpieces in those same museums? And aren't they masterpieces because they so embody the people's whole personality and culture that they are not even signed, and do not need to be signed? We never think of the individual artist who did the work, but of the kind of society that could produce such works.

We must work for two things: paintings that can hang in Black institutions where they can be experienced as a part of our history, and the same art reproduced in posters, books, or other forms.

Reproduced work is a means of reaching *all* the people with positive Black images and information. We must surround Black children with Black images, in classrooms, recreation centers, and homes. We need inexpensive reproductions by hundreds of different Black artists whose works cover the full spectrum of the Black experience. Then children will see artists not as an exceptional few, but as part of the total Black community. It will be easier for them to see art as a natural part of their daily experience.

There will develop, I feel, an ideology which will make artists one force among others in the Black community. Artists will *complement* —not compete with—each other; one artist will pick up where another leaves off.

It is my belief that Black artists can achieve meaningful social objectives by forming cooperatives, such as Nyumba ya Sanaa (House of Art) in Harlem. By pooling their resources in a common fund, they can support the group and permit its members to produce their best and most meaningful work without the worry of earning a living. Once the group begins to distribute its inexpensive reproductions to the community, it is self-supporting and able to carry on its valuable work.

Langston Hughes, one of our most prolific and loving Black artists, was a perfect example of one who shouldered his responsibility to the people by taking his work to them. He would collect from his publisher a quantity of his books of poetry, rent a car, and take them to the South, reading in churches and schools and selling at cost or giving away his books.

There have always been Black people who have given back what was given to them, and passed it on so it could live forever. What is most important is that it reinforces our identity with our group.

During my student days I showed in my work what I really felt about the harsh reality of Black life in the United States.

In the early 1960's, I felt that Black people would be turned off by work that showed the impact on them of raw oppression. I thought that we needed to see the beauty in ourselves that had been denied. So I tried mainly to reflect beauty, ignoring pain. I chose this path for my own sake as much as theirs.

Later, in Africa, two Senegalese artists who saw my drawings of African-American children asked, "Why do they look so unhappy?" I **69**

then realized that I had not hidden the pain at all. I now know that Black people see and feel whatever I put into my work, whether they want to or not. In the faces of those Black children of America, I showed both bright hope and despair—beauty, and the ugliness of oppression, the *complete* truth.

Out in those same streets I drew in every day and night there are slums, inferior schools, unemployment, police brutality, thieving merchants, hustlers, rapists, sellouts, old and young drug addicts, pushers, pimps, and muggers. Too often when we see this in pictures we want to turn it off because it is ugly. It reminds us that we lack control over our life and destiny and are, therefore, still slaves.

But *we are not responsible for the ugliness.* We did not create the conditions under which we have lived. We are not yet free, and our artists must keep telling us that truth. "Black is beautiful" should not serve as only a slogan which keeps us from seeing and dealing with our real condition.

Yes, there is joy in the Black community, too—we have held onto our humanity thanks to our African souls, and that has helped us to survive. But survival is not enough; now we must live.

The life style that comes out of mere survival should not be mistaken for "culture," for it could lead to romanticizing misery and could cloud the truth of our situation. Black people sing the blues to ease the pain of oppression; it is the music of an oppressed people.

Our artists and writers should take care not to lead us into seeing it as "art" or "soul culture." Real culture comes from a people who are free.

One of the most basic things I have learned in the past ten years is the importance of what is best for Black people the world over, the importance of the collective.

No Black child should have to go through years of soul-searching, self-doubt and struggle just to build up his ego enough to withstand the onslaught of racial oppression. More Black people fall in the struggle than survive it.

70

Those of us who survive and even become "successes" should not allow ourselves to be held up as proof that other Black people could do the same, if they really wanted to. Nothing has changed for the masses of Black people. And we should not begin thinking of ourselves as superior individuals. For we know, or should know, that we are just a part of a creative, talented people.

If we survive and manage to accomplish something, it is due less to individual drive than to a spiritual force, to our African souls. We should not permit ourselves to think that our strength as a people came just from our experience in America. It was passed on to us, through our parents and grandparents from our African forefathers. This spiritual force is collective.

Each generation must, out of relative obscurity, discover its mission, and fulfill or betray it.

Frantz Fanon. From *The Wretched of the Earth*

As I see it, the only ideology that will liberate Black people is one which involves the linking up of African people throughout the world, all working together, instead of in isolation.

I believe that the struggle for control of our own communities and learning skills is a positive thing. But how can we expect to build an Africa in a land where there are 180 million white people to our 40 million, where the struggle can only be for a "job" and for "equality?"

I have written this book knowing that my family and I are going back to Africa, by way of Guyana, in South America, where there is a cooperative Black government working toward a cooperative society. This is the same route in reverse that many of our people were *forced* to travel. We are returning *willingly*, lending our services in Guyana before going on to Africa.

My heart is with the Black people of America, but my soul is in Africa. My going will not leave a hole, for I am only one individual. And what we Black artists are building, I hope, is a force of artists who will someday feel that their collective work so embodies Africanness that there will be no need even to sign it. We will simply be giving it back to Black people.

71

I say to our young people: while you are young, travel if you can. See as much of the Black world as possible. Go to the Caribbean. Go to Africa, to the source of the spiritual force that helped us survive 400 years of forced labor and oppression, where Black is not only beautiful, but natural.

America is not the world, and American values are not the only ones, as young people who go to Africa will see. If you want to go, learn a skill that you can use. There, where you are in the majority, and where there is *real land,* you can work together to build a free nation.

It will not be easy. It is much easier to *talk* nationhood here in America. Real nation-building is not romantic; it is hard, sometimes dirty work.

Many of us who have already been in Africa must go back now and help develop that great potential source of power so that Black people, wherever they choose to live, will be protected. We must go willing to work and fight incessantly to build a strong Africa—because it is ours and we love it, and because without it, no Black people anywhere on earth will ever be really free.

72